I0469702

Keeping Honey Bees and Swarm Trapping

A Better Way to Collect "Free" Bees

Grant F.C. Gillard

Keeping Honey Bees and Swarm Trapping
A Better Way to Collect "Free" Bees

Grant F.C. Gillard

Copyright 2012 Grant F.C. Gillard

ALL RIGHTS RESERVED
No part of this publication may be reproduced, stored in a retrieval system, or transmitted, in any form or by any means--electronic, mechanical, photocopying, recording, or otherwise--without prior written permission.

For more information:

Grant F.C. Gillard
3721 North High Street
Jackson, MO 63755
gillard5@charter.net

Grant F.C. Gillard has been keeping bees since 1981. He speaks at bee conferences and conventions across the nation. Contact him at gillard5@charter.net to check his availability.

You can find more information about him at the conclusion of this book, or www.grantgillard.weebly.com

<u>Dedication:</u>

This book is dedicated to the
Wednesday Night Writing Class
taught by Linda Culbreth.

www.bookdesignbylinda.com

I gratefully dedicate this book to her unselfish
leadership and her unfathomable generosity as
she taught and shared a great deal of hard-
earned knowledge. She astutely modeled what
she taught and kept us accountable.
I think of her as my "coach."

With her help, I've become a published author,
yet without her class, I'd be nothing but a writer.

I am also grateful for the participants of the class
who inspired me with their work and their
friendship.

"Give freely and become more wealthy;
be stingy and lose everything.

"The generous will prosper;
those who refresh others will themselves be
refreshed."

Proverbs 11:24-25

Keeping Honey Bees and Swarm Trapping
A Better Way to Collect "Free" Bees

Table of Contents

Welcome!

This manuscript is Part II of my previous work, "Free Bees: The Joy and Insanity of Removing and Retrieving Honey Bee Swarms."

My earlier manuscript, available at my author page at www.createspace.com/4107714 covers the dynamics of the natural swarming process, and how a beekeeper can intercept that process and get some free bees.

That earlier manuscript, technically Part I, covers how the swarming impulse starts, how it builds, how the swarm leaves the hive and how you can catch them. You'll also find tips on how to thwart your own hives from swarming on you!

My practical intent in that previous manuscript was to show you how to get on a swarm call list so people will call you, then how you can arrive at the site to remove the bees and put them to work in your apiary. I detail how to approach that anticipated phone call (and the questions you should ask so you're not coming to "save" a nest of hornets in the ground). I also share how to get those bees into a hive body and put them to work so they'll produce you some honey.

And the beauty of chasing swarm calls is the free bees.

Well, almost free.

There are instances when you don't get to the swarm site in time. While you're on route, the scout bees have found a great place, then convinced the other bees in the swarm cluster to follow them, and the swarm leaves.

Sometimes they leave just minutes before you arrive. Then I find I've invested time and energy and a gallon of gasoline for nothing. It is that very feeling of frustration that moves me to take my swarm chasing to the next level and consider swarm trapping.

This manuscript, "Swarm Trapping" is the follow-up to the manuscript on chasing swarms.

Swarm trapping is another aspect to free bees that entails catching that runaway swarm even when I'm not around and in places I can't always be. I've had my share of experiences where the swarm departed for some unknown destination, and then I've wondered about the swarms that come out of bee trees in remote areas where no human being was able to discover them and call me. And what about the swarms that people find but they don't know who to call? Eventually those swarms will leave for a hollow tree or somebody's garden shed. How can I get those swarms I don't even know about?

Then I began to think about creating some kind of a temporary location that would attract the scout bees so I wouldn't necessarily have to be present to retrieve the swarm, or if I arrived a minute too late, how I might still catch that swarm by setting a trap over the hill or in various locations around the community?

Think about it. You get a swarm call. The swarm has left the hive and is clustered on a rose bush in someone's yard. There's a scared and nervous homeowner who wants the bees removed right now. The scout bees are out looking for a new location which they can call home. The scout bees are searching diligently as you ask some simple questions over the phone about how high the swarm is and how long they've been there. You get organized and start to drive to the swarm site.

As you drive to the swarm location, the scout bees begin to narrow down their criteria for the best site. You hit a red light at the intersection. The swarm cluster begins to unwind and take off. You pull over for a funeral procession on the highway. The swarm cluster flies away to a tree about a half mile from the swarm site and they begin to fill the knot hole in a hollow tree, unbeknownst to anyone in the neighborhood. No one has seen them enter that old tree. You pull up to the swarm site.

The nervous homeowner, still in a state of shock as he witnessed the unwinding swarm, mutely points to the few stranglers, the confused scout bees that missed the swarm's departure for the new site. And you realize you're about five minutes too late. You curse the red lights you refused to run (probably a good thing!).

So you sit around for a few more minutes and visit with the homeowner figuring the whole experience has been nothing but a waste of time. You can't begin to explain to the homeowner what really happened. They wouldn't understand. You vainly scan the sky hoping the swarm is still around. The homeowner wants to know where they went to, hoping they left for somewhere else. But you're not really sure. All you really know is they are gone and you have nothing to show for your interest.

And so you leave with that empty feeling of being a day late and a dollar short. Again.

I've had so many of these experiences over the years that I got to thinking on how to create a box, an artificial cavity to mimic a hollow tree that would attract the bees so I didn't have to be everywhere at the same time. I could space out several of these boxes around the county to catch those bees that get away. I could have a dummy hive, a bait box to attract those swarms that no one sees. It would be a decoy box that would house the swarm until I found time to check it and move it at my convenience.

Once the swarm finds the box and moves in, I could take down that box and transfer the bees to a hive body in one of my bee yards. I wouldn't feel rushed to transfer the swarm and hope they stayed in the bee hive in my bee yard.

And what about those remote and rural areas that no one visits, how a colony swarms from one old tree and takes up residence in another? And how about those swarms that move into someone's house or the garden shed where the siding has pulled away from the stud wall? I hate doing cut-outs.

I got to thinking: how could I put up some kind of trap, some kind of artificial container to attract those bees before they decided to leave for a hollow tree or somebody's garden shed? Could I pre-empt the process of another "cut-out"?

Instead of a cut-out, it would be a simple transfer so this box or artificial container should be large enough to hold conventional frames. And how could I take that box home, simply transfer the frames and start keeping bees in it?

So I began working on this idea of trapping swarms. It wouldn't necessarily be a trap so much as a temporary residence. But how do I make these boxes attractive to the scout bees? (I'll cover that later.) Where would be the best spots to place these traps? (Yep, I'll get to that as well.) And if I could devise a box that would hold conventional frames, wouldn't that make the transfer to a normal hive body easy? (Absolutely!)

I concluded that if I could attract a swarm to move into my trap, then I could move this box with the bees to a bee yard, transfer the frames and set them up in a normal, Langstroth configuration. Then I wouldn't have to be so harried and hurried to rush to the swarm scene. I might actually enjoy a leisurely drive knowing my swarm traps are up and working 24/7. And I could place my traps around the county and catch swarms that no one ever sees!

If you have not read my previous work on "free" bees, I recommend it as a "Part I." "Free Bees" will give you an idea and the background on why honeybees swarm and how you can catch them.

This manuscript, "Part II" is to take you to the next level, to set out boxes that attract those inquisitive scout bees and invite the swarm to move in. These boxes are baited with frames of wax foundation, pheromone lures and set up in such a way as to attract those swarms you can't catch, and swarms you never knew existed, swarms no one sees and swarms that get away when the nervous homeowner is clueless as to whom to call.

Trapping swarms is kind of like fishing. You set your bait and wait for the swarm to "bite." Sometimes you get some "nibbles" from scout bees. Sometimes you reel in a great swarm and there will be days you come home empty.

But the good news is the trap is up to catch swarms 24/7 and especially when you are not around. And it's a lot of fun!

How Do Swarm Traps Work?

The concept of trapping swarms is very simple. The title, however, of "trapping" swarms brings up some strange ideas of fatal mouse traps (a quick and "humane" death) or even those "have-a-heart"-style wire cage traps that keep the animals contained but healthy.

A swarm trap is not really a trap. It's a box, a bucket, a drum or some other attractive cavity that represents a temporary home for the bees. If you are familiar with beekeeping, a five-frame "nuc" box is often used to "trap" a swarm. If you can imagine a five-frame nuc box nailed to the side of a tree or tied onto the lower side of a large branch, then you have an idea of the simplicity of a swarm trap.

There are two, key characteristics of swarm traps. First, they are temporary, and second, they are made to be attractive to the scout bees. Its attractiveness is based on the size and volume, defendability (the entrance or opening should not too large), height off the ground and smell. You can use any box or cavity, and the most popular, commercially made swarm trap available in the supply catalogs looks like a wood-fiber flower pot.

I prefer my traps to look like boxes so I can place standard-sized brood frames in them. The swarm moves in and begins to draw out the foundation and the queen starts laying eggs. With box-style traps, I can take that swarm trap to the bee yard and transfer the frames of brood and bees to a normal hive body.

The transfer process is not difficult which makes a box-style swarm trap ideal.

During the afternoons, I usually drive around to the places where I've hung my swarm traps. I'll notice whether the trap is empty, being visited by scout bees, or whether a swarm has taken up residence. If the trap has a swarm, they have begun to draw out comb, gather nectar and pollen, and the queen has started to lay eggs. Since I don't necessarily visit my trapping sites every day, the swarm may be in my trap for a week to ten days. Because I have conventional frames in my swarm traps, I don't have to check them every day, nor do I have to be in such a hurry to empty the trap.

As far as designating these cavities as a "trap," the bees are not really trapped. They move in, take up residence, draw out comb, then come and go as they please bringing in pollen and nectar. There are no queen excluders, or if you read my previous manuscript, queen "includers," so the foragers have access to come and go and any virgin queen can leave to mate.

Traps offer the best of all worlds because the bees decide to move in. They don't have to be shaken over the trap, only to have another, competing site take precedence. Once they move in, they don't abscond. Once the bees start drawing out comb and caring for brood, transferring the frames to a Langstroth hive body virtually guarantees they won't abscond.

I check on my traps during day-light hours on the sunny days when the bees are flying. That's the easiest way to check my traps. When a trap is full, I make a note to come back after dark, or at sundown at the very earliest. By sundown, most of the field bees are home.

Now you could approach the swarm trap in the early morning, but you have to arrive prior to sunrise or the bees are already working. My goal is to take down the trap with the maximum number of foragers inside.

If I come in the morning, I have to show up in the dark, before sunrise. If I want to arrive at evening, most foragers are calling it quits as the sun sets. Then I have the residual twilight to take down the trap and do my work. There will still be a few foragers coming in, but fewer than if I try and arrive in the morning.

And, of course, if I wait until total darkness, all the foragers are home, but it's hard working in the dark or even by flashlight. My strongest preference is to show up right at sundown.

After sundown, I place a ladder on the tree and climb the ladder to get the swarm trap. Sometimes the entrance has a few bees milling around, guarding their new home. So I stuff the entrance with a paper towel or cover it with duct tape. There is only one opening to this swarm trap, and by plugging the entrance, no one can escape.

Since all the bees are inside the trap, there is no need for a veil, though I sometimes take gloves for comfort rather than for protection. On rare occasions, I'll find quite a grouping of guard bees around the entrance. If I give them a very small puff of smoke, they are more than happy to go inside the trap.

Now sometimes I've been fooled. Some days there are so many scout bees visiting my swarm trap I think I've got a swarm. So later that night, I have learned to climb the ladder and put my ear to the side of the swarm trap. I listen for the buzz of bees. If there is no buzz, I go back home. The scout bees I saw during the day have returned to the swarm cluster and tomorrow will be another day of evaluating sites.

Sometimes there are enough scout bees buzzing that make me think there is a swarm, but by lifting the trap off the nail, I can detect by the weight whether or not I have trapped a swarm. The trap will be heavy if there are bees present.

Studies have also shown that scout bees will investigate potential sites prior to the swarm leaving the mother hive. I may find a few bees milling around the entrance (scout bees guarding their potential location), but a few bees does not mean I've got a swarm. And the beauty is there is no rush to take the trap down. If there are only scout bees present, the trap still has potential to be chosen by the swarm in the next few days.

Confirming the presence of a swarm in the trap, I close off the entrance and bring the trap down and set it in my van. When I know I have a swarm trapped, I'll bring along another fresh, empty trap and put it up in place of the one I just removed. This way I can catch another swarm on another day, and if I bring it along, I don't have to make a second trip, get the ladder out, etc. This means I always have a few empty traps in my garage waiting to be put up.

I suppose, if I didn't want to have any extra traps or I didn't care to spend the money on more boxes and traps than I immediately needed, I could take the swarm trap home with the bees, empty it, then bring it back on another day. But that would mean a second trip and more time. It also means I leave a window of a couple of days when there is no trap present—and that's a lost opportunity!

But sometimes I've got so many bees in so many traps that I don't have an empty spare trap and I end up making a second trip, anyway. And a second trip, made during day light hours, also gives me an opportunity to check the other traps in that area.

But let me digress for a moment. I was visiting with another beekeeper who had two hives. She had a brood box and two medium supers on each hive. She harvested honey from the top super and left everything else for the bees. When I was visiting with her about catching swarms and the need for extra boxes, extra frames, extra bottoms and tops, she looked at me incredulously. "You mean you have all that extra equipment?"

I looked back and said, "Well, yeah. If you want to catch swarms, you have to have that extra, idle equipment sitting around in the event you catch a swarm. You have to have empty boxes and frames already assembled as you need a place to hive the bees when you catch them."

She went on to explain how she bought her hives as kits out of one of the supply catalogs and they were very expensive. I buy used equipment, invest a lot of time fixing and repairing it, and I also scrounge dumpsters for old lumber and packing crates. I make most of my equipment on a simple table saw. I always have extra boxes sitting around. She couldn't believe I had all those extra boxes. I said I need the extra boxes because I'm always catching swarms.

This was a difference of philosophy. She wanted to grow and have more hives, but she didn't have any extra equipment and thought the price was too high to have this vacant equipment sitting around with the hopes of catching a swarm or two.

I keep vacant equipment around with the sure and certain expectation I'll be catching a swarm to fill it. This is true as well for swarm traps. If you only want to make one trip out to this location, then you need empty traps sitting in your garage to replace the full trap you just took down.

And then when you empty this trap into a conventional hive, you can refill it, reuse the pheromone lure, and catch another one. It all depends on how many swarms you hope to catch and having the extra, vacant equipment on hand to accommodate those swarms.

But I digress. Back to our business at hand.

I also place a couple of traps in each location to give the scout bees a choice. In some locations, I will have three traps up and only catch one swarm during the entire swarm season. One could argue that it would be better to place the other two traps in two other entirely different locations to increase the odds of catching a swarm. I prefer to place a couple of traps in each area as bees will have options on which trap seems to suit their needs the best.

Okay. The sun sets. It's dark and I've brought my trap down from the tree. The entrance is plugged and I've replaced it with a new trap. One trip and I've taken down a full trap, replaced it with a new, restocked trap, and I only have to mess with the ladder this one time.

Still under the cover of darkness, I drive to my bee yard and remove the trap from my van and place it on a hive stand. And since it's dark, it behooves you greatly to have that hive stand ready and leveled before you bring the trap home! I have several traps so I have several hive stands in specific yards leveled and all set up to take in a swarm. I set the swarm trap on the hive stand. Then with one swift move, I pull the paper towel or remove the duct tape and run back to my van. "Run" is the operative word.

Since it's dark, the bees won't be flying. But a mass of bees will come crawling out, and if I'm using a flashlight, they will fly toward it. In the dark, bees love to crawl. So if I stick around for any length of time, they'll fly to the light, land on my shoulder and crawl down the neck of my shirt. If I stand too close, they'll crawl up my pants leg. The best advice I can give you is to pull the tape off and retreat quickly to your vehicle. Let it sit for a couple of days.

I'll let the trap sit for a couple of days and give the bees an opportunity to reorient themselves to this new site. Then I'll come back, give them a little smoke, and remove the lid to the swarm trap. I'll transfer the frames to a standard Langstroth hive body and put the hive body where the trap was on the hive stand. I'll gently shake any bees still in the trap into the hive body.

Then I'll set the empty swarm trap about ten feet off to the side and allow the remaining bees to find their way back to the new hive body where their trap formerly sat. Sometimes I'll just thump the empty swarm trap on the ground in front of the new hive body to remove the last remnant of bees.

This transfer is usually done on a sunny day when most of the field bees are out flying. Since most of my swarm traps are six-frame nuc boxes, I need to add four more frames to the new hive body. At this juncture, I don't think it really matters if the additional frames are wax foundation or drawn comb. Drawn comb would have an advantage, but swarms are motivated to grow. If the swarm is large or especially vigorous, I'll add a medium super. I may or may not feed it, depending on the size and stage of the development and where we are at in the honey flow.

As I come back to the bee yard and check on these bees, I will add another medium super. Early swarms will make honey, all things being equal. I also monitor the queen to see if she's old or still vigorous. I want to make sure she's laying eggs. And at this juncture, I'll mark the queen with a dot of appropriately colored paint. I use Testor's model paint and you can pick it up, in just about any color, from any hobby store including Wal-mart.

And this is another digression: the topic of queen quality in a swarm. The general consensus is swarm queens are no good, too old and of unknown pedigree. I have found, based on my experience, that these queens are good and productive. They had to be productive enough to produce enough brood to initiate the swarm impulse. I had some genetic testing done on several colonies of swarms. Almost all of them tested positive for Italian and Carniolan heritage. I have no Africanized genetics in my bees.

If there was one drawback on swarm queens and their suspected quality, it would be their longevity in my hives. I find the queens in the swarms I catch are productive and really lay a bunch of eggs when first hived. They tend to slack off earlier than an Italian queen when fall weather hits. They stop laying eggs in late September or early October when other, commercially-produced queens will continue to lay eggs up into November.

I also find them to be good for that first year in which the swarm is caught, then by fall they are usually superseded by the bees. If they are not superseded, they tend to be a disappointment the following season.

How do I know they are superseded? Because I mark my queens. Let me digress a moment further in that I firmly believe everyone ought to mark their queens. Marked queens are easier to find in the colony, and a marked queen will always be identified on the color of her year. Different years mean I have different colors of paint. I seldom keep queens very long anyway, but when I see her color, I know how old she is.

If the colony swarms or if they supersede her, the unmarked status of her successor lets me know something has changed in the colony. And if the colony has replaced the queen, then I know I have a young queen and the colony won't need requeening.

In terms of swarm queens, I generally leave the marked swarm queens with the colony and I'll either replace her with one of my home-grown queens that I raised that summer or I may requeen the colony with a purchased, mail-order queen if they are still available. While I'm raising 90% of my queens, I still order new, mail-order queens to interject some new genetics into my home-grown queens.

If I like their characteristics, I may leave the swarm queen until the following season, then use her as a breeder queen to raise my own queens.

My bottom line is simple and non-negotiable: Mark your queens. And given today's supply catalogs, you can find a clamshell-style queen catcher. They have tubes with sponge plungers that allow you to hold the queen easily for marking. And they have "paint pens" that make marking easy.

There is no excuse for unmarked queens. If your queens are unmarked, then you have no idea if the queen is too old and at fault for a colony's decline. There are times when some of my beekeeping buddies haven't kept up their mite control. So they end up blaming the queen.

These beekeepers spend a good deal of money on a new mail-order queen, then go through all the motions and risks of introducing her and getting her accepted. And then a month later the colony crashes and they wonder what happened. Usually the producer of the mail-order queen gets blamed for sending the beekeeper a bad queen.

And if you counter my point and complain how you cannot find your queens, start early in the spring before the population gets out of hand. They're easier to find and you can mark them. Or if you buy queens, mark them before you install them. If you raise your own queens, mark them as they leave the mating nuc. If you find your colony has swarmed, the population of workers will be reduced to make finding the queen easier. The longer you procrastinate, the harder it is to find your queen.

And trust me as well on this note: sometimes it's very, very difficult to find that queen, even in a small population of honeybees. If you search a hive and can't find her, let it go for that day. Come back another day. Sometimes searching for that queen leaves the colony so upset and disrupted, it becomes impossible to find the queen. Come back another day, but don't give up and complain to me how you can't find her. Imagine, when the population increases how hard it will be to find the queen. Mark the queen at your earliest convenience.

But I also return to the old standby excuse. If you're just keeping bees for fun and have no concern for their productivity, if you don't really care about the return on your investment of time and energy, then all this talk is moot. If you are happy with whatever you get, even if your hives fail to produce a single drop of harvestable honey, then I'm talking to the wrong person. If you don't really care and are satisfied with mediocre results, then don't worry about marking your queens.

But if you want honey to sell or have honey to show off to your relatives, then step up to the plate and put in the work the bees demand. If you want to make some money and show your spouse** (see my note, below) why bees were a good investment, then put the work in to produce the honey.

> **Note: *My wife was never crazy about my hobby of beekeeping in the beginning. One year, I worked hard and sold enough honey to send her on a Caribbean cruise. She even let me come along! Since that time, she has become very supportive of the time and energy I invest in my bees—and mark my words, it is an investment that pays great dividends. But if you're not willing to invest, there is no pay-out at the end of the season.*

I want my bees to be productive. Beekeeping is extremely profitable and lucrative if you give it the attention it deserves. If you don't give it the necessary attention, then your results will be far less than the potential that exists within every bee hive.

I can almost guarantee you that a dollar of time and energy invested in a beehive will return ten dollars of honey. But again, I digress.

What Kind of Traps Do You Recommend?

You can use any box of any volume to catch swarms. You can hang a five-gallon bucket or an old stereo speaker box (after removing the speakers). I've seen swarm traps made out of old dresser drawers and packing crates.

However, tests have showed that bees have a preference for traps with volumes of 31 liters. These volumes are measured in liters because it was our U.S. government who did the research and they do everything in metric measurements.

So how big is 31 liters? In English measurements, it's going to be roughly 8 gallons, roughly guessing at four liters per gallon, a liter being close to a quart in volume.

To be precise, a liter is .264 gallons, and a gallon is 231 cubic inches. Thirty-one liters is 1890.5 cubic inches and that is also equivalent to 1.094 cubic feet. A cubic foot is equal to 12 inches x 12 inches x 12 inches.

To give you a rough idea of comparable measurements, a Langstroth brood box is 9 and 5/8" tall, by 14 and ¾" wide, by 18 and ½" deep. That's 2626.42 cubic inches on the inside. To divide by 1728 (the number of inches in one cubic foot) you come up with 1.52 cubic feet.

A medium super is 6 and 5/8" tall, by 14 and ¾" wide, by 18 and ½" long and that comes to 1807.8 cubic inches or 1.05 cubic feet.

So you have 31 liters, the ideal volume at 1.094 cubic feet, a brood box at 1.52 cubic feet and a medium super at 1.05 cubic feet.

So this mythical 31 liter measurement is somewhere between a brood box and medium super in volume. I have used conventional, five-frame nuc boxes, and even five-frame nuc boxes made of cardboard (also known in the industry as M.D.A. "Splitter" boxes).

Some of the swarms I've caught have been too big for

these five-frame boxes and while the swarm moved in, I had gobs of bees hanging on the outside of the box. This makes it very difficult to move the box!

You can buy swarm traps or you can make them. I made most of my swarm traps to be six-frame nuc boxes. I made them out of 1 by 12 inch shelving board. The inside dimensions were 18 and ½" long, by 8 and ½" wide, by 11 and ¼" tall. Doing the math, these cubic volumes came to 1769 cubic inches or 1.02 cubic feet.

I think it's fairly important to have the volume of your swarm trap be taller than it is wide, and the only reason I think this is because I'm trying to think like a bee and mimic a hollow tree. Even in cavities that were larger than the 31 liters, bees seemed to prefer a cavity that is taller/longer than it is wide. I presume this is because they like to build their comb vertically rather than horizontally, but that's just my opinion.

Now you can use any box that comes close to these measurements. If you are in a region that is populated by the Africanized Honey Bees (AHB), studies have shown that they prefer a smaller cavity. We don't know why, just that as the government researchers were doing the research, AHBs showed up in the smaller traps and European bees in the larger traps.

You can utilize any box that comes close to these dimensions, but I will STRONGLY urge you to utilize a box that is cut to hold brood frames. If your box holds brood frames, it will make the transfer easier.

What if I Don't Want Frames?

Well, you sure don't have to have frames. One of the commercial traps available looks like a large flower pot. It's described as a "cone"-style trap distinguishing itself from the "box"-style traps.

I have a cone-style trap and I keep it in a place that I can check every day. Once a swarm moves into your swarm traps, they have an urgency to draw out comb and make the place suitable for the queen to start laying eggs. Immediately, once that swarm moves in, forager will be bringing nectar and pollen back. Storage space is needed. Those worker bees want to make that house into a home for their new baby sisters right now!

I've caught a couple of swarms in my cone-style trap and the game plan is the same as a box-style trap. I wait until dark, then plug the hole. I move the trap to a bee yard where I want the colony to go to work. With a cone-style trap, I'm much more rushed to get them out of the trap and into the normal, Langstroth hive.

So I'll go at night, plug the hole and drag the trap to a bee yard. Then the next day, once the sun is shining and the bees are flying, I'll go back out to my bee yard, remove the lid and shake the bees into the hive body.

Bees don't really like to be shaken, and as they are trying their best to get that new home organized, I just mess it up. And I'll also shake out a couple of plates of newly formed, and very fragile, lily-white honey comb. And it's so fragile and thin it just cannot be wired into a frame. What a mess.

There are those who can make those cone-style traps work. I just don't like them. I much, much prefer the box-style traps. In fact, I may just give my cone-style trap away to a friend, but as much work as it is, I'll like give it away to someone I don't really like!

So What Kind of Trap Do You Use?

I will almost always recommend a box-style trap. You can make them out of any material that will tolerate the weather. I've made boxes out of wood, though they tend to be kind of heavy as you carry them up and down the ladder. I've made shelving out of shelf brackets and wood, then used cardboard boxes for the trap. Cardboard is good, easy to work with, but often lacks the right dimensions for frames.

I took some one-bushel apple boxes from the grocery store during the fall of the year when apples were in season and the grocery store couldn't wait to give those boxes away. A bushel, by the way, is 2150.42 cubic inches or 1.244 cubic feet. This is the equivalent of

35.26 liters or 9.31 gallons – well within the framework of the suggested volume.

But the apple boxes were not set up to hold frames. So I made a little frame, kind of like a scaffold, to sit inside the box to hold the frames. I made it out of 1x2" pine furring strips, but it could be made out of any lumber. All it has to do is suspend the frames. I was able to put eight frames in the box.

Since I want a box to suspend frames, it has to be at least 19 inches long on the inside. I've found some boxes that just needed a frame rest glued to the ends and the frames rested just fine. Cardboard boxes are becoming increasingly difficult to find as most grocery stores take the boxes in the back and run them through a crusher that binds all the boxes in a bale for the recyclers. And today, a lot of places use box cutters to remove the lid, then they slice down the sides to remove the items for stocking.

I've looked into buying boxes and there are several moving companies and truck rental agencies (like U-Haul, Ryder) that will sell you boxes. I searched on-line and there are also several companies that will sell you "containers" (the key search word) in any shape and volume. The only downside is they require a volume purchase, and once you pay for shipping, you might just as well buy a five-frame nuc box.

I've gotten longer use out of cardboard boxes by covering them with a trash bag before setting them on the wood shelf that holds them to a tree.

Five-frame nuc boxes work, but tend to be a little small. But they will work. Several beekeeping supply companies now sell a cardboard, five-frame nuc box. Cardboard is fine, but the weather tends to cause them to quickly disintegrate. I've tried them and found they need a cover. I even tried painting cardboard boxes with enamel paint and even bees wax. When it comes to any kind of coating, they are like sponges. They really soak it up and then they don't last appreciably longer than unpainted cardboard.

The M.D.A. "splitter" boxes come in a waxed cardboard. The web site is, **http://www.mdasplitter.com**/. These traps tend to hold up much better than regular cardboard, but after one year in the Missouri summer, they tend to fall apart the next summer. These five-frame boxes also tend to be too small to fully handle some of large swarms they've attracted.

I made my nuc boxes out of scrap lumber, and to utilize a full board of my scrap lumber with the least amount of waste, I came up with a six-frame design. The scrap lumber was 1 x 12" shelving boards to the height was 11 and ¼" tall on the inside. I use ¼" plywood for the top and bottom. I think one of the advantages of making my own traps out of 1 x 12" boards is the extra space under the frames I garner over the standard 9 and 5/8" brood box.

Once upon a time, you could buy wonderful, wood-fiber, box-style traps. They were molded and held together with an asphalt adhesive—very weather resistant. They were marketed for a brief time by Brushy Mountain Bee Supply. But the boxes had lids that warped and beekeepers complained. Many traps were returned to Brushy Mountain, and they contacted the manufacturer, Western Pulp. Then Brushy Mountain told the beekeepers to take the complaints directly to Western Pulp.

Legend has it that Western Pulp got tired of the complaints, so tired that they quit taking phone calls. I contacted Brushy Mountain about this problem stating I had no problems and that I really liked the traps. They said they had several hundred traps on the loading dock they couldn't sell (because of the complaints) and they couldn't return (Western Pulp wouldn't take them back).

I called back asking if they would sell me those unwanted traps, hoping for a discount. By the time they got back to me, the traps were gone. I wrote Western Pulp and they simply said the traps were no longer being manufactured. No further information was offered and no further messages were returned.

And that's their respective stories and they're sticking to them. Suffice it to say, the traps worked great, held five frames, and the bees loved them.

But now they are history. Too bad. I still have most of my wood fiber traps from Western Pulp. They're starting to show their age after twelve seasons. Squirrels love to gnaw on them. Mice like to nest in them when they're in storage. I've repaired a bunch of them with strips of cardboard and 8-mesh wire. The bees will work the inside and begin to smooth the wood fiber, but for the most part, these traps were ideal. I'm not sure why the company caved in to the complaints.

All of these box traps need some kind of support to hold them to a tree. I've built wood shelves that the traps sit on, and with my wood nuc boxes, I've screwed in a simple 1 x 4" board that sits higher than the top of the nuc box.

If you want to view some pictures of different trap designs, designs that I've used, you can access a web page of my own creation at

http://www.feralhoneybees.homestead.com

As you look through the pictures, you'll find the link "Next Design" about in the middle of the page. You'll also see how the wax cardboard, M.D.A. "Splitter" Box began to warp and I tried to fix it with duct tape.

The last thing to remember in the size and dimension of the swarm trap is to create a hole, preferably around 1-1/4" in diameter drilled in the lower portion of the front of the trap.

What Makes The Trap Attractive?

These traps have to be attractive to the honeybee. As the scout bees go looking for competing sites, a good swarm trap needs four basic components.

The first component is size and volume which we've just discussed. The second component is smell. The old timers who made swarm traps (calling them "decoy" hives, "bait" hives, "catch" boxes, "dummy" boxes) made them with different and unspecified dimensions. They didn't have the government research recommending 31 liters. Still, they would scrub the inside of the swarm trap with a fist full of peach leaves or the leaves of a wild cherry tree. Some would find an herb called "lemon balm" and rub these leaves on the inside.

I've also found it helpful to install frames of new, fresh smelling wax foundation. Beeswax has a great smell. It has also been recommended to hang a frame or two of used, drawn brood comb. The smell of old brood is supposed to attractive as well. The downside to used brood comb is that it's also attractive to wax moths.

In my part of the country, southeast Missouri, I generally don't have a problem with wax moths until the end of the swarming season in July. The simple solution is to take down the traps before the wax moths move in.

If you have a used frame that has some propolis on the end bars, it's even better. Propolis is an attractive smell to the bees. Drawn comb is also helpful for the swarm to get an early jump on storing nectar and space for the queen to lay eggs. Also attractive is a used nuc box, with bits of old wax and propolis in the corners. It just smells like home to the honeybee.

All of this is helpful, but the best way to get a nice smell to the swarm trap is to hang a swarm lure. The supply catalogs sell swarm lures that are created out of synthetic pheromones. These pheromones mimic the smell the bees give off from their Nasanov gland. This is the pheromone the bees use to convey the best location of the prime nesting site.

The catalogs sell a lure that may come in two different vials, encased in a paper envelope. Leave the vials in the envelope and simply tape or thumbtack the paper envelope above the opening, on the inside of the trap. The smell of the lure will permeate the plastic tube and give your trap three months of attraction. Pop the top on that tube and the lure will evaporate faster and you'll reduce it's effectiveness to two weeks. Most lures last all season long (about four months from mid-April to mid-July) so I simply buy new lures every spring.

I've experimented with synthetic lures and I've had good success. Several suppliers carry the lures and they're all good. If I had to pick my preference of suppliers, contact Great Lakes Integrated Pest Management at **http://www.greatlakesipm.com** and ask for item #SC-L311, the European Honeybee Swarm Lure.

In a moment of frugality, I've also saved the tubes from year to year and refilled them with the essential oils of lemongrass oil, palmarosa oil and lemon myrtle oil. Some trappers will just rub a little lemongrass oil across the top bars and close up the trap.

Glorybeefoods.com and **Camdengrey.com** offer essential oils if you cannot find them by a simple Internet search. You can find these lures in small quantities at your local health food store.

In terms of their efficacy, old frames and peach leaves will have a 10% effective rate. A swarm lure has a 90% rate. Swarm lures cost between $2 and $5, depending on quantity and shipping costs, and they are well worth the cost. One caught swarm will pay for ten lures.

There are other lures on the market, but they are not really lures. You can buy little tubes of Q.M.P., which stands for Queen Mandibular Pheromone. It basically smells like a queen. I've never used it, though other trappers feel it works in conjunction with, and enhances the presence of a synthetic, nasanov pheromone lure. These are also available from most of the beekeeping supply houses.

The <u>third</u> component, after size and smell, is where you hang the trap. Most trappers suggest you hang the trap 8 to 10 feet high. I've found the most productive trapping locations are sheltered areas along fencerows and creeks. Wooded areas work good, close to open areas like fields and pastures. The trap should not be hung in open areas that get full sun. But hanging them in a fence row alongside an open area is ideal.

There are some people who are adamant that the opening of the trap should face south. Others suggest it should face east. Some compromise and say it should face southeast. I'm not sure it makes a big difference. When I find a sheltered area, I hang my trap in a wooded area, on the shady side of the tree, about ten feet from the edge of the open area. I point the opening toward the open area.

I've also experimented with multiple traps in one site. The direction of the opening has not yielded any conclusive results. I have not found it matters which way the opening faces. I have, however, found that the larger the tree on which you hang your trap, the greater your chances of catching a swarm. You increase your success by hanging the trap close to the fork or crotch in a large tree. The bees instinctively know that forks and crotches in a large tree often yield access to a hollow spot in a tree trunk.

The suggested height of 8 to 10 feet is not set in concrete. I've walked into woods where the creeks flowed and the landscape was anything but flat. I've walked into brushy areas that would make dragging a ladder an impossibility. So I carried a swarm box into the woods and simply hung it as high as I could (which given the terrain was shoulder height) as I stood on the ground.

And these traps have worked.

Interestingly, I've set up a bee hive on a hive stand with a standard brood box, ten frames of drawn comb, and topped it with a medium super (and the ten frames of drawn comb). These hives sat in full sun. They were only a foot off the ground. These were winter dead-outs I set up to be ready to receive a swarm. And to my surprise, when I brought a swarm out to set in these dead-out hives, I found a swarm had already moved in.

Some years these "dummy" hives have caught feral swarms. Some years not. Some locations have and some locations have not.

What I really want to show is the bees will do exactly what we say they won't. They fool us and make a fool out of our logical ways of thinking. We think we know what the bees need and what they want. And then they do just the opposite. Don't worry if you cannot hang the traps 8 to 10 feet. If anything, get some traps set out, bait them with a lure and old comb and hope for the best.

In my old age, I'm becoming increasingly "land-locked." I like to keep my feet on the ground instead of climbing ladders. And it's not the height that I'm afraid of—it's that abrupt stop at the end of the fall that really makes me wonder if climbing ladders is a wise thing to do.

When a swarm moves into a trap and has a week to draw out comb and store in-coming nectar, that trap gets heavy. Bringing it down a ladder is tricky. No swarm is worth the medical and rehabilitative costs of falling off a ladder.

And lately I've become less worried about vandals stealing my traps. Hanging a trap ten feet off the ground deters vandals and thieves, but lately I've moderated my stance in favor of keeping my feet on the ground.

The top three components to trapping swarms is 1) volume and design; 2) smell; and 3) location and height. The fourth component is the network of locations.

By the "network," I mean where the traps are located in a larger scope and how many traps you put in each location, and how close the location is to an adjacent location. I like to find my sheltered areas for traps and I'll hang two, maybe three traps. These traps were hung on different trees in different spots within that sheltered area, all about ten feet from each other.

Then I'll find another sheltered area at least two miles away from this site. The swarm lures were supposed to draw swarms in an area of one mile in all directions from the trap location. I feel two or three traps increase the effectiveness of that location, intensifying the location in that larger, one mile radius. Moving down the road two miles (or more) means my trapping areas won't overlap. This will enlarge the territory covered by the swarm traps.

It has been said on numerous occasions that trapping swarms is a lot like fishing. There are some days the fish are biting like crazy on certain baits. Come back the next week with the same bait and you can't catch a thing. Your favorite fishing spot may work for two or three years then suddenly the fish have moved elsewhere. I move my traps around, and I still have a few spots where I always catch some bees. Then each year, as I add a new bee yard, I'll hang some new traps in new areas in the event my hives would swarm.

So where should your areas be? How do you get started finding a prime location? I've often caught swarms or did cut-outs and have the nervous homeowner say, "Is there any way I can keep the bees out of here or keep them from building a colony in the wall of my garden shed again?"

That's when I suggest there might be a mother colony somewhere close. The likelihood of more swarms in subsequent years is fairly good. And if I did a cut-out, the homeowner's anxiety is higher. They don't want another swarm moving into their house or garden shed. That's when I suggest a swarm trap might be a good idea.

We find a suitably sheltered area, out of the direct sun, in a place where we (both the homeowner and I) can keep an eye on the trap and remove the bees once they are caught in the trap. Technically, as I explain the concept to the homeowner, the bees are not "caught" as much as they "move in" to the trap. Sometimes I need to give them the assurance that no bees are hurt in the "trapping" process. Most people don't want to kill the honeybees.

I sometimes set traps around my bee yards to increase the likelihood that if my hives swarm, I might increase the likelihood of catching my own swarms. I'll find areas within a maximum of one mile of my bee yards, and generally set the traps no further away than ½ mile from my bee hives. But much depends on the locations and where traps can be set, or more specifically, who will allow me to set traps on their property.

I think bees, as they swarm and look for ideal spots, will move as far away from the mother colony as possible in order that their respective foraging areas won't overlap. Logically, why would they want to compete with the hive they just swarmed from?

Schmidt and Thoenes (1990) discovered European honeybee swarms will typically travel 250 to 500 meters (less than ½ mile) before finding a new homesite. There is a belief that a swarm that moves out will want to go far enough away so they don't compete with the mother colony, but like all conclusions, there are exceptions.

I was once called to perform a cut-out in a garden shed in a densely wooded yard. The shed was simply constructed out of a 2 x 4-framed stud wall with ¼" plywood on the inside and 5/8" rough-cut plywood on the outside. It appeared like a squirrel or maybe a woodpecker had gnawed or chipped two holes in the exterior siding. One hole was on the south side of the shed and the other hole was on the east side. The owner of the property called me to say he had this massive bee colony that was "coming out of two holes in my shed." The shed was probably 10' by 10' and set on a concrete pad.

As I removed the siding, I discovered two separate bee colonies, each holding their own in the walls of this shed, each within six feet of each other on different sides of this same shed.

So much for our "knowledge" that bees have a logical sense to choose a nesting site more than a mile from their previous home so their forage area doesn't overlap. And judging by the size and age of the comb, the colonies had been in that shed for a couple of years.

Do Swarm Traps Work?

My first foray into swarm trapping happened about fifteen years ago. I saw, in the Brushy Mountain Bee catalog, an offer for a video tape on trapping swarms using swarm traps. They sold the swarm traps and the swarm lures. I bought two box-style traps and two lures.

The traps were heavy and the shipping was expensive. I think I paid $16 dollars apiece for the traps and $2.95 for the lure. With the shipping, I had around $25 or so invested in each trap. At the time, you could buy a package of bees for around $24 plus $8 to $10 for shipping/postage. It seemed like a fair trade-off, but there are no guarantees with trapping swarms.

I hung one trap off the corner of the church parking lot, in a small, wooded area on the lower edge of a hill. It was a sheltered, wooded lot next to a residential neighborhood. The other trap was hung in the middle of one of my bee yards.

The first week in June, having the traps installed for about a week to ten days, BAM! I caught a swarm in the trap off the church parking lot. I thought this was great. I moved the trap to a bee yard later that night, transferred the frames to a Langstroth hive the next day, refitted the trap with fresh frames and hung the trap in the same location on the following day. I reused the same lure leaving it in the trap.

The next week, BAM! I caught another swarm in this same location. At first I thought, "Heck! This is like shooting carp in a barrel." And in all honesty, I've never shot carp in a barrel and can't for the life of me figure out why anyone would want to or how that opportunity would find its way into anybody's schedule. Nonetheless, I was delighted.

And I began to conclude this was so easy it ought to be illegal!

So, after two weeks, I had two swarms, that if I had bought as packages, would have cost me around $88 dollars. I had around $50 or so invested in swarm traps. The traps paid for themselves after the first two weeks.

Then the morbidly negative thought crept into my brain: Do I have enough hive bodies, tops and bottom boards to hive all these hundred of swarms I'm going to catch this summer?

As fate would have it, I must have irritated the benevolent grace of the swarm deities. My other trap did not catch any swarms nor did I catch any more traps at that location off the church parking lot for the rest of that season. But that was only one summer.

The next summer I bought fifteen more box-style traps and caught more swarms in different areas, as well as another swarm in the church parking lot. That's when the nice people at Brushy Mountain started receiving complaints about the warping lids and it wasn't very long before these traps were unavailable.

There was another year I repeated my procedure and hung a swarm trap in this same location off the church parking lot. The tree in question was a pecan tree and of substantial size. I initially pounded a nail into the tree (which some people conclude is a horrible sin) and hung the trap about 10 feet off the ground. I had caught a swarm in this trap each of the previous years. I was ready to catch another swarm, or two, this year.

So as this particular spring started out, I hung a swarm trap in the same place with great optimism and expectation. About ten feet away was an aging silver maple tree.

As the summer progressed, the neighbor complained that the maple tree was dying. It was actually on his property but the canopy straddled both the church parking lot and his yard. He called a tree trimmer to come and cut it down and the tree trimmer found a colony of honeybees had taken residence. The tree trimmer would cut it down but they looked to me to remove the colony before the tree could be cut up into manageable chunks.

The tree trimmer was great to work with. He dropped the tree and let me use his chain saw. Judging by the color of the comb, this was not a long-established colony. It might have come from the previous year or maybe not. It could have been an early swarm from that particular spring. What impressed me was how the bees chose a hollow tree when just ten feet away I had given them the perfectly sized, perfectly scented, perfectly placed swarm trap.

Sometimes things just don't work out according to our logic.

An Alternative Use for Swarm Traps:

I was called another time to remove a swarm from a hollow tree. The tree was fairly small, but it looked like the hollow spot ran the length of trunk. There was an opening close to the bottom of the tree and another about six feet up. The tree was, at most, twelve inches in diameter and the bees were using both entrances.

I cut down the tree and dragged the trunk about ten feet away. I set a swarm trap on the stump. This trap was set with five frames of wax foundation, one frame of open brood borrowed from an existing hive in one of my bee yards (removed just minutes before I left for this cut-out) and a swarm lure. I also made sure the queen was not on the frame I borrowed from the existing hive, but I did make sure there were some young bees and fresh eggs.

The beauty of a swarm trap is that it's temporary and so it's easily moved and transported. As I dragged the tree trunk away from the original site, a host of field bees came back to the stump where I placed the swarm trap and began entering as if it was their own home.

I commenced to cut up the tree trunk, and it was obvious the comb they built in this narrow hollow spot was not suitable to wire into frames. So I kept cutting the tree trunk into manageable chunks about 12" long. I'd shake the bees out in front of the swarm trap, and the bees would fly around and begin their trip back to the closest thing that smelled like home. The bees orient more on location than they do with other factors.

With each section, I'd bang out the bees as I thumped the log section in front of the trap. I carried these log sections back to a bee yard and let the bees rob out the honey. I came back three days later, after dark, and plugged the hole and brought the trap to its permanent location in a new bee yard. The bees took the frame of brood and made some queen cells (obviously I missed or killed the queen in the tree). Two weeks later I moved the frames to a normal hive body. By the end of the summer, the hive was doing fairly well for such disruption.

Swarm traps are meant to be temporary and they work either to hive the bees from a cut-out or can be used to pick up a swarm as it's brushed off a rose bush or mailbox. Or if you do a cut-out, a swarm box can be used to collect the stray bees as they fly back to the original site.

A Success Story:

I had a great experience one summer morning. I got a swarm call to retrieve a swarm hanging on a storefront overhang (canopy) in downtown Cape Girardeau. It was another busy morning for me, personally, and when I got the phone call, I promised I would be right there, as soon as I was able, to come and pick them up.

As I visited with the caller, asking the questions a good swarm catcher ought to ask before racing to the scene, the swarm had come to rest on the overhang of a store front that morning. The overhang was about eight feet above the sidewalk and the police had strung that yellow tape that says, "Police Line: Do Not Cross."

And as swarms go, it attracted quite a bit of attention.

My departure from the office took more time than I wanted and by the time I got my swarm retrieval equipment ready and got myself down to the swarm site, the police were taking down the tape. The swarm was gone.

There were still a few scout bees flying around and they explained to me that I was "just two minutes too late." I just missed the swarm and I cursed my bad luck of not being ready with my swarm catching equipment ready to go at a moment's notice. I couldn't tell if the police were irritated that I didn't make it in time or that the swarm got away...or both.

Bystanders told me tales of how the swarm started falling to the ground like someone was pouring water. Only when the bees hit the pavement, they jumped up in flight. They started circling, whirling and the noise was incredibly loud. And then the air was filled with this swirling cloud of honeybees, then it was like the skies cleared and the bees disappeared.

It's fun hear their side of these stories as you'd think there was some kind of plague of biblical proportions. The innocent bystanders share these stories as if I'd never seen or heard of bees taking off in flight from a swarm cluster. I knew what happened and gauged their stories as a little bit of an exaggeration, but I nod respectfully nonetheless.

Then came the questions from the bystanders of where those bees went, where did they come from, what would you have done with them, will we see another swarm, how long have you been keeping bees?

After about twenty minutes of conversation, I sense the need to leave and get back to work. Everyone thanks me and I tell them to give me another call if they see another swarm. I hand out a few business cards for good luck. Maybe someone will call me for another swarm. For me, it's just another one of those experiences of being just minutes too late.

Since I'm in the area, I decided I'd take a look at some of my traps I have located close the riverfront in Cape Girardeau. The first trap I approach is three blocks away from the swarm site. It's actually a block west and two blocks north. The owner of the house had an older home, and typical of older homes, the woodwork at the corners, under the eaves, along the soffits had begun to rot. The previous summer squirrels chewed a hole in the corner and the next thing he knows, he had bees living in his house.

He didn't want bees living in his house.

He called me that previous summer to come and remove the bees, but this roofline on this old house is thirty feet in the air. The pitch of his roof is like 90 degrees—it's way too steep for me to be fooling around trying to remove honeybees. In my humble estimation, a bee rescue was just impossible.

So after I balked at the cut out, he hired a professional roofer who killed the bees and fixed the damage. But since he doesn't want bees in his house again, I suggest we hang a swarm trap in the backyard. He thinks it's an excellent idea. The location of the trap is on a large maple tree, about six feet off the ground where the first large branches begin to fork. It's also out of sight of the nosy neighbors.

But the previous summer resulted in no swarms moving in. I figure because it's later in the summer, there would probably be no swarms but it gave the homeowner a little piece of mind. The swarm trap also cemented our relationship, kept me in his mind as the local beekeeper, which allowed me to put up a trap for the current summer.

It's now the current summer and earlier in the spring I had put up a new swarm trap in his backyard. He would phone me from time to time to let me know we had not caught any swarms. He would also inspect the eaves of his old house and let me know no more bees had moved in.

I've now missed the storefront swarm so I drive around the corner and head on over to his house. I figure, as long as I'm in the area, why not check the traps. As I come up to the house, the owner is in the backyard, staring up at the tree where the swarm trap is hung. I get out and walk over. We greet each other, and he says, "It's the darnedest thing. I was out back here watering the flower pots on the patio, and suddenly the air was filled with bees."

"About thirty minutes ago?" I inquire.

"Yeah. Made a heck of a racket, buzzin' like the sky was on fire. And then just like someone put a vacuum in that swarm box of yours, they all get sucked into that little hole on the end. The whole mess of them just rushed right in."

We both stand there in the yard. Most of the bees appear to be in the trap, but there's probably another hundred or so still flying around like they can't find the entrance. Or maybe they're beginning to orient themselves to the location.

The homeowner says, "So you reckon you got the queen?"

I nod contemplatively. "I reckon so. I'll be back in a day or so, at night, and I'll take those bees back to my bee yard."

Now it's his turn to nod contemplatively.

Was this the swarm from the storefront? I think so, though there is never anyway to really tell for sure. The timing, the proximity, the availability...it's just too perfect to be coincidental.

So This Is Perfect, Right?

No, this is not the perfect method. But I like it. I received a call from an apartment complex where a swarm had clustered on a third-floor balcony. I came and vacuumed up the swarm, took it home, no big deal.

As I was putting the swarm into my truck, the management of the apartment, the security staff and the maintenance staff all wanted to know how to avoid this from happening again. I tried to think of some cutesy, humorous comeback, but I couldn't...and they were very serious. They were thinking of this concentration of humanity in the apartment complex and the issues of liability and public safety.

So I mentioned the idea of a swarm trap in the fencerow along the far edge of the property. I mentioned we could hang the traps about ten feet off the ground to keep curious children at bay. I was going to continue mentioning the advantages and benefits, but before the words came out of my mouth, they all said, "Sure!"

The apartment complex was hedged by a large "L-shaped" line of trees that grew in the fencerow. I placed three traps in the trees, all about ten feet high (mostly to keep them out of reach of curious kids). Every year I catch a swarm or two, and what's funny is the swarms always go to one of the three locations. It's not just that I have three traps in the area, but the swarms show a distinct preference for one of those three placements.

Even as I rotate traps in and out, and even as I mix up traps every season, there is one of those three spots that always seems to be a proverbial "sweet spot."

I raise this example to show that other beekeepers have set up traps, then complain to me how they never catch any swarms. There seems to be a missing factor other than being the right volume, having the right smell, set at the right height, etc. There is something in the landscape, the topography, the angle of the sun that the bees pick out as a preferential selection factor.

And I have no idea what it might be. I've even taken the other two traps and moved to them different locations in the tree line. And the bees continue to show this one spot as their favorite.

It's not perfect and there is no foolproof method of catching and trapping these swarms.

What's the Season for Swarming?

Well, this will vary from region to region, obviously. For me, in southeast Missouri, our swarms start right after the dandelion bloom, about the middle of April. If you read my earlier manuscript on free bees, it is the warm weather that excites the queen to lay eggs like crazy. Warm weather also means a surge of nectar and warm weather allows foragers to collect that nectar.

The competition for the in-coming nectar along with the demand for more egg laying space causes congestion, and congestion is the leading cause of swarming. Swarming starts when the weather final settles down and there is a reliable source of nectar and pollen.

And likewise, when the nectar and pollen cease, and the queen slows down her production, swarming will also decline. I see our nectar flow quit around mid-July. Swarm calls pretty much drop off and my swarm traps start attracting squirrels and wax moths (if I've been using old, black comb). If you don't use old, black comb, wax moths will not be an issue.

I make it a point to put my traps up in late March and early April (before I get busy with swarm calls) and then I start taking them down in late August after my busy time of extracting supers tapers off. I open the traps, cull and sort any comb into storage boxes, then put my traps into my winter storage.

There have been a couple of times I left traps up all year, partly out of negligence on my part, after all, we only have so much time during the day. Then I wondered if I just left them up in the spring, would I catch a swarm? They never caught another swarm the following year. It pays to take them down, replace the lure, clean out the spider webs and mouse nests.

Swarm lures will last about three months. I order them in January, then store them in the refrigerator. The traps go up the first part of April, and I calculate the lures last through April, May and June. So what about the swarms that I might catch during the first part of July?

Have you not heard that a swarm in June is worth a silver spoon but a swarm in July isn't worth a fly? (Or is it "let it fly?")

Late swarms always seem to need a lot of T.L.C. Late swarms never seem to be overly motivated and often come loaded with Small Hive Beetles. Early swarms are much more ideal. By the beginning of July, I consider any swarms I might catch as requiring more work. Certainly their potential is limited to preparing for the next year. They definitely need feeding, but they are still free. I never look a gift horse in the mouth. Still, I'm not about to worry about whether or not those lures are still up to their potency for that last stretch of the swarm trapping season.

How Far Do I Have to Move the Swarm Trap Before Putting it in a Hive?

Once you catch a swarm in a swarm trap, you'll need a new location and move the swarm to a hive body. If you don't move the swarm to a hive body, they'll quickly outgrow the swarm trap and then it will, first, become an intractable mess, and second, it will like produce another swarm because it outgrew the swarm trap.

I'd like to deny I know anything about this problem, but procrastination and problematic weather, coupled with a busy schedule, all seemed to conspire against me. Once the bees enter the trap, when I make my rounds to check on the traps, I try and get them down ASAP. I move them into my bee yards at night, and give them a couple of days to orient before I shift them over to a Langstroth hive body.

In my first years of swarm trapping, I tried pulling down a swarm trap (one placed in the middle of my bee yard) and setting up a hive about twenty yards away. I couldn't understand why the bees kept flying up to the tree where the trap was and why they would cluster up there and not in the hive where the queen was at. So I would sweep up those bees into a bucket and dump at the new location where I set up the hive body.

It didn't take me very long, and I'll bet you already can guess where this is going, that you need to take down the trap and set it on a hive stand more than two miles away from the trapping site. The bees choose the swarm trap as their new location. They start orienting immediately on that site as their new home.

Merely moving the swarm trap to a hive stand several yards away does not reorient them correctly. They'll always fly back to the site of the swarm trap. And if you take down the old swarm trap and put up a new one, they'll move into the new trap. You may even think you caught another swarm.

If you put a swarm trap in the middle or even on the perimeter of your bee yards, you need a new location to set them up in a hive stand that is more than two miles away. Not everyone has these second or third bee yards, but you need to keep this in mind if you set up a trap in your bee yard. Alternatively, the lesson is to set your trap somewhere else more than two miles away from your bee yard, but then you lose the advantage of potentially catching your own swarms.

I set the trap on a hive stand and give the bees a couple of days to settle down and reorient themselves and I have no problem with foragers staying home. Transferring the frames from the trap to a new hive body is no big deal as newly trapped swarms are still very gentle.

Some FAQ's:

"Don't swarm traps around your bee yards encourage your hives to swarm?" No. Swarming happens inside the hive. Swarming is a natural response triggered by congestion and crowding. You can't entice a colony to swarm by hanging something outside the hive. The stimulus to swarm happens internally.

"By catching swarms, or bees that are 'swarmy,' aren't you collecting bees to put in your hives that will swarm next year?" Not necessarily. Swarming is an instinct written into the honeybee D.N.A. All honeybees will swarm, some races more than others, some races less than others. Some years are more swarmy and other years are not. Swarming is an instinct that you can reduce through sound management principles. It is not

necessarily a behavior defined by previous years, but be warned that some races of bees are more swarmy than others.

"I'm new to beekeeping and I cannot afford to buy a package of bees. Do you recommend a swarm trap so I can get started with free bees?" No. You cannot schedule a swarm and late swarms do not perform as well as early swarms once you hive them. There's no way you guarantee you'll even catch a swarm with a swarm trap. It would be better, if you were starting out, to sacrifice the money and buy a package, then start trapping swarms for expansion once you get the hang of keeping bees.

"Where can I get some traps?" I will adamantly stand by my opinion that box-style traps are the only way to go. Any trap I use, whether purchased or home-made, must hold conventional frames. This alleviates the pressure to move the trapped swarm ASAP and facilitates the transfer PDQ. (Don't you just love acronyms?) Unfortunately, the only traps available for purchase through the conventional beekeeping suppliers are the cone-style traps. This means you need to either buy some home-made traps or make them yourself. Alternatively, you can convert five-frame nuc boxes to

swarm traps, but I think these boxes are a little small to adequately attract and hold a swarm.

"Do I really need a swarm lure?" No, but it increases your chances of catching a swarm by a factor of ten. You are ten times more likely to catch a swarm with a lure. They may seem expensive, but an empty swarm trap is even more expensive in terms of the lost opportunity.

"What if this idea of trapping swarms just seems like too much work and I don't want to go around putting up traps?" No problem. In your bee yards, or in places where you would like to set up a new location to keep bees, set up a level hive stand. On the hive stand place a brood box and ten frames of wax foundation. You might even add a medium super with its own ten frames of wax foundation. You might also include a few frames of old, drawn comb and I would highly recommend a swarm lure.

Now sit back and wait. Sooner or later, you stand a good chance of catching a swarm or having a swarm move into your vacant hive set up. Now I don't think you're going to maximize the opportunity to catch a swarm, but this is probably the lowest input, least cost method of catching a swarm—and it will work.

Other Resources to Consider for Beekeeping:

Check my author page at www.grantgillard.weebly.com and click on the tab that says, "My Books."

Here are some highlights.

"Beekeeping with Twenty-five Hives" is for the beekeeper who wants to take the hobby of keeping bees to the next level of producing surplus honey. This e-book details how to find new yards and locations, maximize the honey production, stream-line the harvest, increase the marketing options and start making some money.

"Making Plastic Foundation Work for You (and your bees)" is written for the beekeeper who wants the convenience and the labor-saving practicality of plastic foundation. However, the bees will tell you how they much prefer the old-fashioned, wire-supported wax foundation. They will normally buck and balk at your suggestions to convert to plastic foundation. This book will show you how to persuade your bees of the benefits of plastic foundation and how you can get the bees work with you, not against you.

"Free Bees: the Joy and Insanity of Catching Swarms" is the topic that really started me into beekeeping. Free swarms gave me the advantage to start keeping bees and to expand while saving money at the same time. This is the e-book if you want more information on how to have people call you to remove those pesky swarms, and in this day and age, there has never been a more advantageous time for beekeepers to offer their services for swarm removals.

###

About the Author

Grant F.C. Gillard is an author and frequent speaker at bee conferences. He began keeping bees on the family farm in 1981 after graduating from Iowa State University. He graduated from Fuller Theological Seminary in 1987 and earned a Doctoral degree from Aquinas Institute of Theology in St. Louis, MO. He combines his passion for beekeeping with his pastoral duties at the First Presbyterian Church of Jackson, MO.

Grant currently operates around 200 hives and produces honey for local sales in southeast Missouri. He traps several swarms each year and selects the best colonies to raise queens from using the NICOT non-grafting queen rearing kit. He markets his honey at farmer's markets and local grocery and health food stores.

He has published several e-books on the topics of beekeeping and personal growth. He has also had several articles published about colony management techniques in the American Bee Journal. A Ton of Honey: Managing Your Hives for Maximum Production is one of his most noted books. He is president of the Missouri State Beekeepers Association and is a frequent regional and national conference speaker. To check on his availability to speak at your conference, e-mail Grant at **gillard5@charter.net**

Check him out, along with a listing of his current books

at http://www.grantgillard.weebly.com

Click on the tab: "My Books"

and you can find him on Facebook and Pinterest, or simply "Google" him on the Internet.

www.ingramcontent.com/pod-product-compliance
Lightning Source LLC
Chambersburg PA
CBHW071247170526
45165CB00003B/1276